Pranayama: The Yoga Breath

How to Transform Your Life by Improving Your Breathing Technique

Sundari Gibran

PRANAYAMA
THE YOGA BREATH

HOW TO TRANSFORM YOUR LIFE BY IMPROVING YOUR BREATHING TECHNIQUE

Sundari Gibran

Disclaimer
Although the author has made every effort to ensure that the information in this book was correct at press time, the author does not assume and hereby disclaim any liability to any party for any loss, damage, or disruption caused by errors or omissions, whether such errors or omissions result from negligence, accident, or any other cause.

This book is not intended as a substitute for the medical advice of physicians. The reader should regularly consult a physician in matters relating to his/her health and particularly with respect to any symptoms that may require diagnosis or medical attention.

BN Publishing
Pranayama: The Yoga Breath
How to Transform Your Life by Improving Your Breathing Technique
© Sundari Gibran, 2021
ISBN: 978-1-63823-018-2

TABLE OF CONTENTS

TABLE OF CONTENTS	5
INTRODUCTION	7
THE HISTORY AND ORIGIN OF YOGA	11
How and when did yoga begin?	13
The evolution of yoga	16
What is yoga?	21
Pranayama	27
WHAT MEDICAL SCIENCE SAYS ABOUT THE HUMAN BREATH	29
The nervous system	30
Respiratory system	33
Types of breath	43
YOGA BREATHING TECHNIQUES	45
What is pranayama and how is it performed?	49
Some breathing techniques for beginners	59
Overview	63
BENEFITS OF PRANAYAMA	65
Benefits for mental health	67

Benefits for physical health	69
Spiritual benefits	70
Benefits for emotional health	72
Benefits of specific breathing techniques	74
The yogic lifestyle	77
The relevance of Pranayama in recent times	79
CONCLUSION SO FAR	81
BONUS: YOGA AND THE DAILY ROUTINE	83
Achieving Samadhi	89
Complex yoga poses	91
YOGA LITERATURE	97
REFERENCES	99

INTRODUCTION

Nowadays, everyone is striving to feel fully alive even if it is only for a few moments. We want all our senses to be recharged after being exhausted for so long. For those who have experienced it, being numb is probably the worst feeling in the world.

It would be a long discussion if we start listing the reasons that led to people feeling so detached from themselves lately. But to explain it briefly, we can just say that we gradually kept drifting away from our spiritual selves for more materialistic gains.

Now, when we realize the damage done to our emotional health, we desperately want to go back to the simple ways of life. We wish to feel everything profoundly. True happiness, excitement, and all kinds of unfiltered emotions.

At the same time, we want to feel calm and peaceful too. We want to stop feeling anxious all the time. Throughout the day, we're either worried about what will happen next or scared that something that went wrong in the past may happen again.

A single solution to all the aforementioned problems would be to spend a few minutes concentrating on yourself. That is, to set aside some time from the busy daily routine and just focus on your inner feelings. And the best way you can do that is by practicing yoga.

Yoga is an ancient technique used for physical and mental fitness. It involves many different positions and postures aimed at keeping your mind and body completely fit. Frankly, regular practice of yoga, if done in the right way, can eliminate many health-related issues from your life.

Although it's not some kind of a substitute for medical science, the benefits it provides are almost equivalent to those of a health tonic. That is why you often see a yoga instructor having the ideal body shape and a calm demeanor that makes you want to try yoga for yourself immediately.

You may have heard the famous quote that the journey of a thousand miles begins with a single step. In the case of yoga, that first step you take also happens to be the most significant part of this technique. Before you can get to more difficult poses, you already feel the difference.

This text is about the foundation of all yoga poses, i.e the yoga breath. Yoga breath, technically called pranayama, is a deep breathing technique that helps calm your nerves. Along with stress-relief, it provides so many additional benefits that you will learn about later in the text.

The phenomenal effects of this breathing technique make it the need of the hour today. With such chaotic lifestyles, we all need a magical solution for our mental and physical health issues. In addition to providing that, yoga breath also helps you connect with nature more profoundly.

Overall, it wouldn't be wrong to say that simple practice helps improve the quality of your life significantly. It relieves the extra pressure from your mind and makes your body a lot more active. Since we're all trying anything we can to survive in this tough environment, something as simple as pranayama is definitely worth a shot.

THE HISTORY AND ORIGIN OF YOGA

Many people have heard of yoga as a form of exercise. Some start doing it to lose weight while others consider it a method of staying active. In the modern world, it has become a rather 'cool' part of an individual's lifestyle.

Yoga classes are now a form of social activity. Online interactions about the subject earn you more friends and admirers. Moreover, it has become a profitable business for those who know a significant deal about the technique.

But only true sages realize the real potential of this ancient practice. Every pose or '*asana*' has a deep impact on your mind and body. It seems like the saints must have mastered this art with a lot of contemplation and insight.

Lately, just like the real form of yoga, the idea of its teacher or '*guru*' has also been hijacked. In reality, a yoga guru isn't just someone passing instructions and explaining physical movements during a workout session. It is a coveted position held by the most devoted disciples of this technique.

The exercise, for the lack of a better word, is easy to learn but hard to master. It requires utmost dedication and determination. At the same time, it isn't something overly technical with a checklist to complete.

It is like a study with no defined curriculum but a clearly illuminated path. A yogi or yogini is well aware of the goals to follow as well as the mental and physical habits to steer clear of. He/she stays vigilant about the teachings not just while performing yoga but generally in life as well.

When we mention the word 'sage' a thousand different images may appear in your mind. Some may perceive it as a person living away from the rest of the world at a secluded spot like a jungle or a cave. Others may know a sage to be someone with a disheveled appearance wandering here and there with no specific destination.

But these understandings have deviated far from the real meaning of the word. Actually, sage refers to an individual with immense wisdom. Sages are known for their sound judgments about different matters of life. People often seek advice from them whenever they are faced with a complicated challenge.

So, by that definition, an experienced yoga *guru* can be called a sage. Historically, it was the sages belonging to different philosophies who developed these poses. And anyone who becomes an expert in the yogic philosophy not only becomes a teacher of practicing yoga but attains the position of being a sage as well.

This is why yoga has an edge over other modern methods of fitness. Each one of its poses has been developed as a result of a deep, insightful thought process. Therefore, every pose has multiple benefits for your mental and physical health.

The effect is so overwhelming that yoga has become a religious practice for many people around the world. It is used as a way of connecting to the spiritual forces of nature. With regular practice, a yogi starts to feel like a part of that nature instead of being alienated from it.

Although this text would mainly focus on a single aspect of yoga, it is important to learn a bit about the background of this technique. After all, you can't just dive right in without knowing the depth of the water. You need to be fully aware and convinced about what you should expect and whether or not it would serve your purpose.

More than a branch of physical exercise, yoga is a way of life. A yogi learns to regulate all his/her emotions without needing any external help. The answers are mostly found automatically when a person spends more time performing different yoga poses.

How and when did yoga begin?

The roots of yoga date back to as early as 3300 BC. It was part of the Indus Valley Civilization and thus believed to have originated in Northern India. But not much about the technique was documented until the mid-1900s.

A common misconception about yoga is that its teachings are exclusively based on the Hindu faith. Although the philosophy is heavily inspired by Hinduism, it also contains elements of other faiths like Buddhism and Sufism. Let us see which parts of these philosophies coincide with yoga.

In the 6th Century BC, Gautama Buddha laid the foundation of Buddhism. His main purpose was to connect the physical form of human beings to their spiritual selves. The main technique he used for this was quite similar to modern-day meditation.

Buddha isolated himself from everybody or everything that could distract him and settled in a quiet, peaceful place. He would then close his eyes and focus on his own thoughts and feelings. Gradually, he learned to detach himself from anything that could force a reaction out of him.

The technique enables the one practicing it to achieve calmness and enlightenment. Most statues we see paying tribute to Buddha capture him in the same meditational position. Along with this, certain other postures also capture the essence of Buddhism.

Similarly, if you have ever meditated, you would agree that the practice temporarily puts you in a trance. It almost feels like you have been transported to a different place where things are a lot more mystical. So, in a way, yoga takes influence from the Sufi practice of trying to connect with the Creator.

The aforementioned examples are meant to highlight the fact that yoga is an amalgamation of different spiritual practices and not derived from any single faith as it is often suggested. According to an article by Malini Nair:

> *Yoga is not a culturally homogenous, all-Hindu, Vedic tradition, as is often portrayed by revivalist demagogues and those who have set up a raucous campaign to reclaim its roots. It is, in fact, a liberal, eclectic tradition that absorbed freely from Buddhist, Jain, even Sufist ascetic practices.*

Citing an academic work titled Roots of Yoga by Mark Singleton and James Mallinson, the article further states that one shouldn't fall for anyone dressing up a certain way in order to appear as a yoga expert. Yoga is for everybody regardless of age, culture, or religion. (Nair, 2017)

One of the reasons that yoga is identified with the Hindu religion, in particular, might be the first theoretic mention of this technique being in Rig Veda. The Vedas are ancient religious texts written in Sanskrit. Rig Veda (which means The Knowledge of Verses) comprises various hymns about Hindu mythology.

Although the exact theology of yoga remains a mystery, we do know that the technique has existed for more than 5,000 years. So, it would have been molded by every generation according to its own needs. As the tradition passed from one generation to the other, it is believed to have incorporated many new influences as well.

The purest or the oldest form is Vedic Yoga. Over the years, the practice developed into Hatha Yoga as we know it today. This further reinstates the notion that yoga has drifted away from its spiritual aspects and is more widely known for its physical postures.

The evolution of yoga

Earlier, performing yoga would require a peaceful, natural environment. You could truly connect with nature in the wild with sounds of birds chirping and a stream flowing nearby. Hence, it was easier to feel closer to one's spiritual side.

Later, technology completely changed the way this concept is perceived. Virtual classrooms can create a suitable atmosphere with ambient music and sound effects. This increased convenience by allowing people to participate in a yoga class no matter where they are physically. But it also made the practice deviate slightly from its pure form.

We're not suggesting that a certain physical environment is necessary for yoga. But since yoga is mostly used to calm the mind, it is best done in isolation and in a natural environment. Once you have experienced that kind of serenity, you wouldn't even think about performing yoga in an enclosed space.

Patanjali is an iconic name in the history of yoga. He wrote the Yoga Sutras, a text which holds the importance of a religious scripture for the followers of yoga. The text is categorized into four main parts namely Samadhi, Sadhana, Vibhuti, and Kaivalya.

The first chapter (or pada) is related to reaching the ultimate state of self-realization. In simpler words, a beginner is told what his/her aim is going to be and what entails on the path ahead.

Ling Beisecker while writing for DOYOUYOGA explains samadhi in the following words:

Samadhi Pada

The first chapter is about enlightenment, focusing on concentration and meditation.

The 51 sutras discuss the process to become One. The sutras define yoga, obstacles to achieving yoga, the purpose of yoga, the importance of abhyasa (constant practice), and vairagya (detachment from material experiences).

Samadhi is considered the last one of the eight limbs of yoga. The first seven that come before samadhi are yamas, niyamas, asana, pranayama, pratyahara, dharana and dhyana. Here is a brief explanation of all the 8 limbs of yoga.

Yama

These are about giving up evils and rectifying your behavior towards others. You vow to be nonviolent, truthful, not steal or waste energy and not be greedy as well.

Niyama

Niyama is about adopting the right principles in life. These include purity, contentment, spiritual observances, study, and devotion.

Asana

Then come the physical postures called asana. These prepare your body to achieve enlightenment.

Pranayama

These are breathing techniques that harmonize your mind and body with the forces of the universe.

Pratyahara

This is about changing the focus from the outer world to your inner self. You become less conscious about the happenings around you and focus on your own conduct.

Dharana

At this stage, the yogi learns the true form of meditation. The level of focus and concentration is enhanced.

Dhyana

Achieving a perfect state of mediation.

Samadhi

Samadhi is when you become one with the divine energy.

Sadhana Pada

The second chapter is about the practice. The Yamas and Eight-Limbed system of yoga are introduced.

The 54/55 sutras outline Karma, Kriya yoga, Ashtanga yoga, and the first six parts of the Eight Limbs of Yoga are discussed in-depth.

Vibhuti Pada

The third chapter is about the results, power, and manifestation once union is achieved.

The 56 sutras clarify the last two Limbs, dhyana and samadhi, as well as introduce the power of simultaneously activating the last three limbs. The chapter begins to highlight the ability of yoga to empower the mind.

Kaivalya Pada

The last chapter is about liberation, or moksha. The 34 sutras clarify liberation and what is achieved by the mind. This final chapter is devoted to complete, unconditional, and absolute liberation.

While reading all of the sutras is suggested, reading and making one sutra pure in your life is enough. The sutras are tools to foster the inner experience and elevate the spirit. Practice leads to wisdom and the ability to allow the inner light to guide the present moment, or atha.

What is yoga?

This subheading does not lay enough emphasis to depict the confusion some people have about yoga. More than being an inquiry about the technique, it is usually an expression of exasperation at the insistence to try it out from one's peers. It seems like a huge mystery to find out what *really* is yoga?

You see, sometimes you hear so much about a subject that it starts to bother you, even though it might be something extremely beneficial. One wonders what the fuss is all about. In other words, being constantly fed with others' opinions about something kind of puts you off.

The problem is, the focus lately seems to be on projecting the good parts of an idea or thing. Whenever someone is advocating an idea, he/she follows a one-dimensional approach. Although this is done to make the idea more appealing, it deprives the process of complete honesty and authenticity.

In this era of marketing, people are only interested in selling an idea. But with things like yoga, making it sound like a superficial, instant solution to all the problems proves counterproductive. When a new follower of the technique does not see any physical change within a few sessions, he/she starts wondering if everything they heard was just a marketing gimmick.

We've all been fooled by overhyped products and services so many times that we do not wish to take another chance. Moreover, we want instant results because we have so many things going on in our lives simultaneously. Hence, we prefer rigorous gym sessions and drugs that produce quicker results.

This is probably the only area where yoga loses its appeal in comparison to more modern alternatives. If you manage to find an authentic guru, he wouldn't hasten the process. He will advise you to spend a lot of time getting into the feel of yoga.

This obviously isn't possible for a commercial yoga class that is only looking to increase the number of students. They want the word to get out and the revenue to multiply. So, they accelerate the process significantly.

Though you still reap the benefits of some of its teachings, the experience is nothing like real yoga. Yoga, if followed properly, is a way of life. It changes you spiritually, mentally, and physically. But the transformation is never instant.

With yoga, you settle into the technique gradually. The peace and calming effect that it brings is a result of immense patience. You don't just change from an erratic, anxious person to a sage overnight.

To put it simply, you must believe in the process and give it enough time. An impatient person might not find this technique suitable as it takes much longer than other methods. But for those who believe that good things take time, the results are also much more gratifying.

There are several types of yoga namely Kundalini Yoga, Hatha Yoga, Bikram Yoga, Ashtanga Yoga, etc. The most well-known type around the world is Hatha Yoga as it combines all the physical movements in the technique. For a beginner, it is not important to be able to distinguish between all the types efficiently.

However, with some prior knowledge of each type, it becomes easier to choose which style you would eventually settle for. You can then narrow down the suitable postures according to your needs. But the basics of the philosophy are more or less the same.

Modern yoga instructors often make the mistake of setting unreasonable standards for new students. They want to inspire and encourage new pupils to push their boundaries.

It is one thing to tell a person about the advantages of a certain pose. But to define how it would make him/her feel would make the experience inorganic. Just to match the teacher's enthusiasm and fit into the crowd, a pupil may not express openly or hesitate to modify the routine as per his/her personal requirements.

A much better approach would be to introduce a person to the technique and let him/her explore it without any influence from another person. For each individual, the effects of yoga take shape quite differently even though it may be equally helpful to everybody.

A guru can at best take the disciple by the hand and send him off into a world of

This is almost like teaching a toddler to walk. You can encourage him to take the first few steps but if you hold his/her feet and improvise the walk yourself, the child would never learn to walk properly himself. So, your guidance should only show him the way and not hinder his progress.

The literal meaning of the word yoga is to unite or combine. It is derived from the Sanskrit word Yuj which means to yoke or to join. The real purpose of yoga is often defined as joining one's own spirit to the spirit of God/universe.

Firstly, this destroys the notion that yoga is just another weight loss technique. Secondly, it tells us that real yoga is also much more than the weekly, half an hour lesson in a studio. Lastly, for the believers of spirituality, it is an extremely intriguing concept.

Being spiritual is not the same as being religious. It doesn't involve well-defined rituals or practices, nor does it consider the people questioning certain beliefs as outcasts. It is like free-falling in love with the universe and its creations, including yourself.

Yoga requires you to consider yourself a small part of the nature. You have to believe that your body is an extension of the same forces that the rest of the universe is made of. A part of it dwells in your soul, which joins you to the rest of the creations in an unbreakable bond.

Thus, when we say yoga combines or unites you to with nature, it means that the technique enables you to dig deep within your soul. You have to keep introspecting until you find that part that is completely pure, undiscovered by the rest of the world. Basically, the technique reconnects you to some part of your original personality.

From birth to death, as we keep aging, the influence of the outside world keeps overshadowing our original personality. Gradually, we become the person that the world approves of, leaving our happiness and inner satisfaction behind. This becomes a disease for our soul as it desperately wants to break free and reunite with the elements it was initially made of.

Yoga also increases the synchronization between all your senses and thus enhances your focus. It eases the process of transitioning from one task to another without feeling overwhelmed. Therefore, we can also say that it combines the different aspects of your personality into a more congruent form.

Moreover, it can bring greater harmony if practiced collectively on the level of society. It has something to offer for all age groups and body types. Apart from seriously-ill patients, it is a harmless technique for everybody.

So, according to the discussion above, yoga is like a cleansing of the soul. It eliminates the impurities that build up over time. Hence an individual gets closer to his higher spiritual self.

Physically, yoga makes you a lot more agile, flexible, and fit. It delays the signs of aging and keeps your skin fresh and healthy. Moreover, with improved blood circulation and breathing techniques, your body feels fresher and lighter.

Mentally, practicing yoga on a regular basis rids you of overthinking. You attain greater control over your emotions and learn to deal with the negative ones in a healthier way. It provides an outlet for all your frustration, anger, and sadness.

Yoga lost followership during the British rule in India. During this time, the groups actively performing yoga became smaller and smaller. The number of disciples within India became insignificant so the rest of the world joining in the technique was out of the question.

However, it was popularized again in the mid 20th century. The gurus took the teaching to different parts of the world. This time, the idea was incredibly well received and spread like wildfire all over the world.

Lately, it has again gained relevance due to the increased stress levels all over the world. As the technique combines mental, physical, and emotional health remedies, it feels like the obvious solution to the challenges that the world is currently facing. After all, you can't feel completely healthy if even one of these aspects remains unaddressed.

Pranayama

Although the main subject of this text will be discussed in greater detail later on, we can't really go any further without at least explaining it briefly. For those who are completely unacquainted with the way yoga works, it seems surprising that all the health effects that we have mentioned above can start merely with a single breath. But this isn't just about any breath we're talking about, pranayama is a full-fledged health remedy on its own.

Pranayama is a part of Sadhana Pada along with yama, niyama, asana and pratyahara. The remaining three limbs are included in Vibhuti Pada.

The literal meaning of prana is life energy or breath. Ayama means to control. So the words combined i.e. pranayama means control of breath.

It is mainly about how one can extend or expand one's breathing. All of yoga's postures are based on this breathing technique. In fact, this is the first thing that you learn when starting yoga.

In her book 'A Beginner's Guide To Yoga' Nancy Phelan familiarizes the new followers of yoga with the basic techniques. While explaining the breathing technique, she emphasizes that we take in prana (the life force) through our pores, tips of our fingers, and mainly through the lungs. But when the breathing is shallow, we do not inhale enough prana.

Generally, the first step of any journey is extremely special. Hence, pranayama holds great significance in a yogi's life. Later, one can distinctly remember and reminisce about the huge difference it made. No matter how much of an expert you become and how many difficult postures you master, this basic technique always has its own value.

We may not acknowledge this often but our respiratory habits play a greater role in influencing our overall health than we realize. For example, shallow breathing leads to greater stress and strained muscles. Breathing deeply helps keep our mind and body relaxed.

Just like yoga as a whole, its branches like pranayama are also misinterpreted as either something overly technical or something completely mystical. For optimum benefits, we need it to be a mix of both. We need the practice to help us practically without losing its magical touch.

Many people are not fully aware of the relationship our respiratory system has with the rest of the body. It affects our nervous system, our mental and physical abilities. So the simple act of inhaling and exhaling properly can prove immensely beneficial for your health.

WHAT MEDICAL SCIENCE SAYS ABOUT THE HUMAN BREATH

To 'breathe your last' is a tragedy. It means that the fire that kept you alive has died down. That your soul has departed from this world.

We try to avoid this tragedy for as long as we can. Getting treatment for illnesses, making our lives as easy and comfortable as possible, ensuring safety and security are examples of the steps we take to prolong our life expectancy. But in our everyday lives, we neglect the very basis of our existence, i.e our breath.

We don't pay much attention to the way we breathe. Quite often, improper breathing techniques lead to health complications that seem completely unrelated. It never occurs to us that a seemingly automatic process may also require more focus.

For any living organism, breathing is an important part of life. A healthy respiratory system ensures better overall health. This is why medical professionals tell you to never smoke, breathe in some fresh air and avoid pollutants as much as you can.

When a person is drowning, he/she desperately wants to come out of the water and breathe freely. It is at that time that you realize what a blessing it is to be able to inhale and exhale without restriction. Otherwise, we're quite oblivious to our lungs mechanically doing the job all the time.

This drowning situation is equivalent to the overwhelming feeling we experience when we're under stress. We want some instant relief from the terrorizing feeling. For a moment, let's put the emotional aspect aside and try to understand why our body reacts so strongly to stress.

The nervous system

Our nervous system is made of the brain, spinal cord, sensory organs, and all the nerves in the body. It is divided into two categories i.e. central nervous system (CNS) and peripheral nervous system (PNS). The CNS is formed by the brain and the spinal cord. The peripheral nervous system comprises all the nerves that connect the other organs of the body to the central nervous system.

Have you ever wondered how your body recognizes different sensations? How does it know when your arm is hurting or your feet are cold? Science explains it in the following words.

'Input from our senses is taken in through the body's sensory receptors, which then convert the input energy into neural impulses. These neural impulses enter the cerebral cortex of the brain, where they are interpreted and organized in the process of perception.' (Boundless psychology)

(Source: https://courses.lumenlearning.com/boundless-psychology/chapter/introduction-to-sensation/#:~:text=Input%20from%20our%20senses%20is,in%20the%20process%20of%20perception.)

Sounds complicated? Let's try to simplify how this system works. Basically, when a sensory organ (e.g eyes, nose, lips, ears, hands, or skin) feels something, our nerves connecting the organ to our brain act as messengers and inform the brain about what has happened. A certain part of the brain then deciphers the message and gives a name to the feeling.

Amazingly, this happens at a lightning-fast speed. Within the blink of an eye, we can say that we just felt pain or that we just enjoyed something tasty. In fact, we can recognize multiple sensations at the same time.

Sometimes the process is simple. For example, when a child falls down and hurts his knee, he immediately feels pain and cries his heart out. The reaction and response to pain are quite clear in his mind.

As we grow older, this clarity gradually diminishes. Instead of letting out an honest reaction, we over-evaluate everything that we feel. Looking at this perspective, it almost feels like children are more emotionally intelligent than adults.

What we mean to say is, for various reasons, our reactions become less profound as we age. The reasons include adherence to certain social protocols, not having enough emotional support as compared to childhood, increased responsibilities, etc. An overly emotional person is seldom taken seriously so we want to avoid being labeled as one, as much as we can.

Hence, to achieve this state of being less emotional, we start suppressing our inner feelings. We go against our basic nature to fit into the crowd. Social validation and approval overtake the need to emote freely.

Along with that, there are some events that are genuinely hard to process. Even though an event may be the adult equivalent of a child falling down in the aforementioned example, we don't realize it right away. We're either too numb or too reluctant to admit being hurt.

For instance, when you're fired from a job, it is definitely a huge setback. But you may not express it openly because you want to put up a brave face for your family or you don't want to make it seem like a big deal. But deep inside, you're really hurting.

This is where our behavior comes into conflict with our inner feelings. Instead of showing sadness we act cool and smile for our loved ones. Or, even if we do express it, it is in a way that would seem socially acceptable.

The state of confusion messes us up more than we realize. In the short term, we may earn praise from our peers and even enjoy momentary success in different areas of life. But this hypocrisy harms our mental health more than anything else.

Think of overstuffing a box with more items than it can hold. You keep filling it without considering the limited capacity and eventually, it breaks. So, instead of gaining something, you end up losing a lot.

Alternatively, when pouring water into a glass, you cannot fill it beyond its capacity. The excess water will just spill out. You won't be able to store more, you'll just waste a valuable resource.

Emotional tolerance varies from person to person. But each person does have his/her own limit. One cannot simply keep piling up emotions and expect not to have an outburst sooner or later.

When that happens, the losses are greater. Years of anger, sadness, and frustration ruins many relationships. The impact is much higher than what it would have been if the issues were addressed at the right time.

Moreover, there's a lot of additional stress in recent times. Increased competition, lesser person-to-person interaction, greater expectations, and whatnot. So, the increase in depression and anxiety is quite understandable.

Respiratory system

The respiratory system includes our lungs, airways, and blood vessels. Its main function is to supply oxygen to other parts of the body. You inhale oxygen from the air and exhale all the waste gases (like carbon dioxide) out from the lungs.

So, it doesn't just keep you alive by supplying oxygen, the system also performs the function of cleansing your body. Proper inhalation is important to provide sufficient oxygen to all your organs. The failure to do so would result in serious health consequences.

Similarly, if you don't exhale properly, the residue of gases like carbon dioxide in your lungs will keep increasing. This will result in impairment of pulmonary function. As lungs play a crucial part in your health and wellbeing, the shallow breath can be detrimental in several ways.

For a moment, just imagine if your breath is limited. Now connect this with the information that you have just read. You probably understand why you'd feel so constricted at times.

Taking a deep breath after a heavy activity is like opening a window to let in some fresh air. It almost seems like you have just stepped into a healthier environment where the air is much cleaner. You can also feel the physical effects almost instantly.

In reality, you're breathing the same air but your inhalation and exhalation have improved. And that effect is similar to an improvement in the air quality around you. Since you're taking in more oxygen and releasing more carbon dioxide, your lungs are more purified.

Let's look at some of the scientific effects of shallow breathing.

Shallow breath causes your heart rate to increase. When your heart pumps faster, your organs do not get enough supply of oxygen. This increases health hazards like stroke and cardiac arrest.

It also explains why you need rest after heavy physical activity. For example, when you go hiking on a mountain, you need to stop and 'catch your breath' after covering some distance. That's because exercise also increases heart rate and the effects are immediately noticeable.

A fast heart is in itself a reason for shortness of breath. So, if shallow breathing has resulted in an increase in your heart rate, you'll be further worsening the problem by continuing to breathe in the same manner.

Understandably, your blood pressure is also higher as your circulatory system is working extra hard. You may have heard that people with narrowed vessels often suffer from high blood pressure. Narrow blood vessels cannot carry adequate oxygen supply to the rest of the body and hence, become more stressed.

Apart from the stress on your internal organs, there's added mental stress as well. Not just because of the discomfort you feel, but another scientific reason as well. Long-term practice of the wrong breathing techniques can lead to higher levels of stress and anxiety.

The scientific explanation for this is that lower blood pressure can help in reducing the stress hormone called cortisol. The presence of more cortisol in the body automatically causes higher blood pressure. So, all of the aforementioned effects of high blood pressure stay relevant to cortisol as well.

Higher levels of cortisol also accelerate the process of aging. Now, that is surely bad news for people investing in expensive surgeries to look younger than their age. Those procedures won't help much if you ignore the other aspects of your health.

Generally, shallow or inadequate breathing lowers your immunity. You feel tired most of the time. And it's even more frustrating when you cannot figure out the reason for excessive fatigue all the time.

Pulmonary health is not discussed as often as it should be. Nor is its true significance explained to the general public. People have developed extremely unhealthy habits like smoking which harm themselves as well as the people around them.

In fact, passive smokers often bear the brunt for no fault of their own. Although the health risks associated with passive smoking are not as high as those with active smoking, there's still a significant threat of developing serious conditions. Inhaled smoke from the environment can lead to diseases like cancer and chronic obstructive pulmonary disease (COPD).

Youngsters in the current generation have one thing in common, they are always in a hurry. They're rushing to get to their next destination, be it a physical place or something they've made a note of in their mind. A fast-paced life may seem exciting for a while but eventually, it gets quite exhausting.

Working hard towards your goal is an extremely appreciable quality. It helps you to stay motivated. It also means that you're passionate and focused.

However, the desire to succeed should never become an obsession. Being too hard on yourself can also be counterproductive. You can fall into despair not just by being left behind by your peers but also by being overly ambitious and failing to meet your own expectations.

The ultimate focus in your life should always be your own health. If you can manage to stay fit and healthy, all other concerns would be secondary. If you feel unwell or stressed, you won't have the desire or energy to focus on anything else.

As we mentioned earlier, this generation is always rushing for one reason or the other. Consequently, there is a feeling of being running in a race continuously. This feeling doesn't allow you to relax completely, even for a few moments.

Now imagine what would happen if you ever ran nonstop. How long would you be able to continue your run? What would be the physical effects of exhaustion and fatigue?

Among other things, you would be hyperventilating. You would be gasping for breath after running more than you can handle. This race we're talking about is equivalent to the current lifestyle we're leading.

Rapid breathing is known as hyperventilation. You take quick, shallow breaths when you're stressed, exercising, feeling unwell, or under the influence of certain medicines. Hyperventilation can cause lightheadedness, fainting, tingling sensation in hands and feet, muscle tension, etc.

Scientifically, hyperventilation occurs when more carbon dioxide leaves your body than is supposed to. As you're breathing faster, more oxygen is inhaled. This causes an imbalance between the two gases in the body.

The complete opposite is called hypoventilation. In that case, your body lacks sufficient oxygen intake and does not release enough carbon dioxide. Again, the imbalance can lead to health issues.

The symptoms of hypoventilation vary depending on how serious the problem is.

Unlike a real race that causes physical exhaustion, the onset of hyperventilation with mental stress is not too quick. It takes some time before your brain feels completely overwhelmed. But once that happens,

Just for context, both the prefixes 'hyper' and hypo are never good news in terms of medical science. The former means a function is being over-performed while the latter indicates that there is a shortage of something. For your body to work efficiently, everything needs to be well-balanced.

Different parts of the human brain perform different functions. For example, the cerebrum deciphers the messages from the sensory organs and controls the body. The cerebellum is responsible for maintaining balance and controlling voluntary movements. Lastly, the brainstem connects the brain to the spinal cord and looks after the body's involuntary functions.

Some people are not fully aware of all these functions. But for the purpose of explaining the relationship between your mental health and respiratory habits, it would suffice to say that all the aforementioned parts of the brain are affected by your breathing. In simpler words, several functions are disrupted.

The central nervous system, consisting of the brain and spinal cord can thus be considered the foundation of your overall health. Not to scare you but an injury/illness of the brain or spinal cord is the hardest of all to recover from. So, these require continuous care and attention.

Again, the spinal cord has several lesser-known functions as well. Along with keeping the body well coordinated, it is responsible for monitoring sensations and transmitting messages to and from the brain. The spinal cord acts as a connection between the brain and the peripheral nervous system.

If you have ever tried guided meditation, you would have heard the speaker tell you to keep your spine straight. Bad posture is a very common problem in recent times. We have become used to weird sitting positions due to the increased usage of gadgets and phones.

The half-sitting, half-laying position in the bed or on the couch, the bent forward posture on the office desk, or any casual sitting position that causes your spine to bend is extremely unhealthy. It does not just affect your physique but also impacts your mental health negatively.

Our tech-savvy generation understands the language of machines and robots better than humans. It needs help from automated machines to tell how their own body is feeling. We have become accustomed to ignoring the signals and indicators given by the body until it is too late.

In ancient times, people could tell you so much about your health just by studying your pulse. Medics would put two fingers on your wrist and read it quite accurately. In some places, this ancient practice is still used as a method of diagnosis.

According to an article in Heart Views, the pulse-taking method has been around for over many thousand years. It has only evolved into technologically-friendly variations but the main source of every diagnosis still remains the same. Here's a small excerpt from the article.

The majority of patients with a cardiac arrhythmia are asymptomatic; this has been so from earliest times. The patient with a cardiac arrhythmia may or may not feel anything. Some patients may complain of "racing heart" or "skipped beats" or may feel dizzy or faint.

Palpation of the pulse was the sole "window" into the heart for 1000 of years until the mid-20th century. Throughout the history of medicine, the pulse was an important parameter in assessing cardiac dysfunction.

Pulse taking is an ancient technique in medicine. There are many historical illustrations of physicians taking the pulse of a patient. Ancient Egyptian,

Chinese, Indian, Greek, Medieval, Arab-Islamic, and modern physicians know the value of examining the pulse. It is part of what we call our "vital signs."

Pulse taking is still an integral part of medical practice today for the pulse is an important diagnostic sign and can be used to prognosticate the course of illness. A physician well versed in "reading" or interpreting the different characteristics of the pulse in disease is considered a "good doctor" in the past; now, only the nurse takes the pulse.

The advances in medical science have surely made our lives easier. They've made diagnoses much more accurate than in the past. But from the discussion above, it seems as if just like the other fields, it has also made medicinal practices lazier.

The purpose of mentioning the ancient technique of pulse reading is that the significance of such indicators was better understood in the best and therefore, toxic habits could be nipped in the bud. Now we might benefit from better facilities but we let things get too far before we decide to take action. The state that has put our mental health in says it all.

When you drink contaminated water, your body's immune system reacts strongly. You get an upset stomach or fever indicating that your body absorbed something harmful. If that is left untreated, your health can deteriorate quite rapidly.

In the case of inhaling unhealthy air, your body reacts in the form of itchy eyes or nose and breathing difficulties. But the more serious symptoms are kind of subdued. This is mainly for two reasons.

Firstly, because we have become used to polluted air. Our body doesn't identify it as being harmful immediately. We keep suffering for a long time before the symptoms become apparent.

Secondly, the symptoms of mental health issues are quite subtle at first. People might suffer from loss of appetite or sweaty palms and brush it off as something inconsequential. So, the problem remains undiagnosed, let alone getting to the root cause of it.

Nowadays, more and more people are suffering from mental health issues. People of all age groups are affected by problems like anxiety and depression. Unfortunately, it has also increased the occurrence of the worst-case scenario i.e suicides in the patients.

At the same time, physical health is also not ideal. With all the advanced health solutions, one would think that we're living with the ideal health. That is for from the truth.

In the past, some diseases were almost exclusive to old age. Nobody would think a young person can have back and neck problems or suffer from hearing loss. Even pulmonary or cardiovascular diseases were associated with old age as your organs become less efficient later in life.

But today, a 20-year-old person is much more likely to suffer from the same issues as a 50-year-old. It seems like people are aging faster, despite human beings having a greater life expectancy. The quality of mental health in particular, for the overall population, has deteriorated significantly.

Types of breath

There are four main types of human breathing namely eupnea, hyperpnea, diaphragmatic and costal. Each of these types is different in the method and function. Let's quickly review what each of these breathing types entails.

Eupnea is the resting breath that we take unconsciously or subconsciously. Hyperpnea is rapid breathing during exercise or other increased lung activities. Diaphragmatic breathing is deep breathing, the one that we're focusing on in this text. Lastly, costal breathing refers to the shallow breathing that we've mentioned as an unhealthy habit these days.

You may find a more scientific definition of these four types on the following link.

https://bio.libretexts.org/Bookshelves/Introductory_and_General_Biology/Book%3A_General_Biology_(Boundless)/39%3A_The_Respiratory_System/39.3%3A_Breathing/39.3B%3A_Types_of_Breathing#:~:text=Types%20of%20breathing%20in%20humans,each%20requires%20slightly%20different%20processes.

Coming back to the diaphragmatic breath and why it is so effective, let's refer to an article published on Cleveland Clinic's website. Explaining what diaphragm is, the article states:

The diaphragm is the most efficient muscle of breathing. It is a large, dome-shaped muscle located at the base of the lungs. Your abdominal muscles help move the diaphragm and give you more power to empty your lungs. But chronic obstructive pulmonary disease *(COPD) may prevent the diaphragm from working effectively.* (*Diaphragmatic breathing exercises & techniques* 2018)

The article explains diaphragmatic breathing in the following steps.

1. Lie on your back on a flat surface or in bed, with your knees bent and your head supported. You can use a pillow under your knees to support your legs. Place one hand on your upper chest and the other just below your rib cage. This will allow you to feel your diaphragm move as you breathe.

2. Breathe in slowly through your nose so that your stomach moves out against your hand. The hand on your chest should remain as still as possible.

3. Tighten your stomach muscles, letting them fall inward as you exhale through pursed lips. The hand on your upper chest must remain as still as possible.

4. When you first learn the diaphragmatic breathing technique, it may be easier for you to follow the instructions lying down. Later, you may also try this while sitting on a chair.

The term is often used interchangeably with the diaphragmatic breath. This is how similar the effectiveness of both these breathing techniques is. So all the benefits of pranayama that you learn later in this text, would also apply to diaphragmatic breathing.

You can say that pranayama takes an edge only because of its spiritual benefits. Otherwise, there are a lot of similarities between both these techniques. In scientific terms, when you're told to breathe deeply, it means you're being advised to adopt diaphragmatic breathing.

YOGA BREATHING TECHNIQUES

The yoga breath takes you to a serene, tranquil environment mentally. The feeling is extremely refreshing as compared to being trapped in a concrete jungle all the time. You may be in the middle of a chaotic workplace and yet feel like you're visiting somewhere pleasant.

The practice provides much-needed relief from all the hustle and bustle around us. It changes your perception of things. When you're relaxed you automatically start focusing on solutions rather than worrying about your problems.

In therapies, patients are often taught the importance of positive self-talk. Even though the inner voice does not have a separate physical presence, it influences our thoughts and feelings just like another person. These thoughts and feelings ultimately affect our physical health as well.

So, it is believed that talking to yourself kindly can help uplift your spirits. The inner voice can increase or destroy self-confidence as it builds a right or wrong perception about yourself. Our perceptions of things can induce physical reactions without us realizing it.

Similarly, shallow breathing sends a signal to the brain that we're in some kind of trouble. It sets off the panic mode in our minds and bodies. Consequently, you start feeling physical symptoms of stress and anxiety.

Our breath gets shallower after heavy physical activity, in fear when we feel nervous or stressed, and in some more similar situations. So, naturally, our brain's perception of shallow breathing is that something is gravely wrong or that we're feeling unwell. This sends it into a fight or flight response mode.

Your lungs, chest muscles, and all related organs have to work extra hard when you do not breathe properly. It tires you out even more. So, that's added pressure for your mind and body.

Another problem with an improper breathing technique is that your body does not get enough oxygen. This, combined with the fact that you don't exhale all of the stale air present in your lungs, creates trouble in the long term. The incoming fresh air decreases while the stale air keeps piling up in the lungs.

It may not have any significant effect immediately. The difference is hardly noticeable. But in the long run, it leads to mental health issues as well problems related to your physical health.

Earlier, we learned about the link between the nervous and respiratory systems. That in itself is explanation enough for the deterioration of mental health with our usual breathing.

Learning about pranayama is like the dawn of a new life. It is like starting to see everything clearly after years and years of foggy vision. You may notice that even the examples that we're using to explain what it feels like are mostly related to nature.

Imagine standing on a beach and watching the sun rise on the horizon. Gradually, the darkness changes to light and everything becomes clearly visible. Even little particles of sand start sparkling as if they've been given a new life.

The main difference between a healer and a physician is that the former uses your own feelings, thoughts, and emotions as a remedy while the latter uses more advanced medical procedures. Yoga is in line with the healing techniques. You don't even need another person to guide you through it, you can be self-sufficient.

The yoga breath requires you to slow down your breathing significantly.

As a result, your heart rate also decreases. The significance of this is that the risk of arteries or veins narrowing or getting blocked is reduced.

The heart rate for a healthy person is between sixty to hundred. For fit people, this number remains on the lower side. Sports athletes are usually extremely fit hence their heart rate is known to be lower than those who do not play any sports. This is what you're trying to achieve by practicing yoga.

It is an automatic process that accompanies different yoga asanas. The more experienced you become in the techniques, the slower and more rhythmic your breathing becomes. Subsequently, the heart rate also follows suit.

Almost every yoga book that you may stumble upon will have a separate section dedicated to different kinds of breathing techniques that yoga offers. Not only is the correct breathing technique an integral part of yoga, but the scientific benefits associated with it enable the followers to feel lighter and fitter sooner than with normal breathing. By normal breath, we mean the very unhealthy form of breathing that is prevalent these days.

For this text, we're using pranayama as a broader term to incorporate all the specific breathing techniques included in yoga. For example, breathing techniques aimed at relaxation, pain relief, better concentration, etc. The crux of the matter remains that your lungs need greater purification for any of these purposes to be achieved.

Prana, the life force or energy is like a nutrient for your lungs and the rest of the body. The first step is to firmly believe that when you inhale, you're taking in all the goodness from the universe. You may imagine it as a light or powerful energy that would make you stronger and healthier as it enters your body.

Similarly, when you exhale, imagine that all the stale air is leaving your lungs. Along with that, all the stress, pain, and any unwanted feeling is also gradually going away. This thought process needs to be repeated with each breath with all your focus being solely on your inhale and exhale.

If you observe your breathing for a few minutes you would realize that we mostly use the upper chest muscles only. Considering the position of the lungs, that means that the air in the lower parts does not move much. When you don't get enough oxygen to the lower parts of the lungs and also do not remove the $co2$ present there simultaneously, it is quite understandable that your lungs cannot work at their full capacity for long.

What is pranayama and how is it performed?

Since this is not a specific posture, there aren't many requirements associated with it. You don't need any equipment or a specific environment for it.

Of course, it would help to have a calm, peaceful place where you can focus only on your breathing. But making this a requirement would limit the scope of this technique significantly. That doesn't resonate with the purpose of yoga.

You may be aware that nature is also called mother nature. And a mother embraces all her children with the same love and affection. It does not differentiate based on their abilities.

Yoga coincides with all the principles of nature. Even this all-embracing, affectionate outlook. Whether you have a disability or you lack physical strength, it won't leave you out of its list of disciples.

The regular practice of yoga breath may be done at your favorite spot in the house or at a different outdoor space every day. You may choose the time that suits you and can do it wearing any attire that seems comfortable. But sometimes, it also acts as an urgent remedy in an emergency situation.

Sounds strange, doesn't it? We're referring to an incident narrated by Nancy Phelan in her yoga guide for beginners.

She mentions that she once received a call from a very distressed female musician the day before her recital on television. The woman on the phone was having a breakdown because she had been working very hard and suddenly couldn't concentrate on anything. She remembered Nancy from one of the yoga books she had read and desperately hoped that she could help.

Nancy called her to her place and sat with her in a secluded spot in the garden. The two practiced deep breathing for more than an hour which helped calm the musician down. Once she was fully acquainted with the yoga breath, she went home with the resolve to continue doing it the next morning and right before her performance as well.

The woman successfully performed in front of thousands of people and attributed this to yoga breath. She later described the technique as lifesaving. Although this might be a little bit of an exaggeration, it is guaranteed that deep breathing is somewhat responsible for alleviating panic-related symptoms.

You see, anxiety or panic attacks are usually accompanied by shortness of breath. Not being able to breathe properly at that particular time worries people further. Since your brain is already overwhelmed with stress, it cannot handle any more of it and suffers a breakdown temporarily.

If one can just manage to stay alert enough to focus on the breath, it would help greatly. Your mind and body would gradually relax from the calming effect of a deep breath. It can make coping with anxiety much easier.

In the long term, the buildup of stress is also reduced. Your body stays in a constant state of relaxation which allows your nerves to work better. Hence, the long-term practice of pranayama can prevent excessive stress and the symptoms associated with it.

In the same aforementioned book, Phelan states that prana is what holds the body together. She explains that the retention and accumulation of prana are the main focus of hatha yoga. It is achieved through various breathing techniques.

Shedding light on these techniques, the author writes:

'The three main kinds of cycles are Recharging Breaths for increasing energy through inhaling prana; Purifying Breaths, for cleansing the bloodstream and emptying out stale air from the lungs; and Pacifying Breaths, for relaxing the nerves, and calming the mind and emotions. There are also breathing techniques for cooling or warming the body, for healing, for use in mental training and meditation. Some of these are only for advanced students but there are plenty of simple and harmless exercises suitable for beginners.'

Before we get into the details about different kinds of deep breathing let's understand the approach for beginners suggested by various authors. The basic technique is more or less the same all around the world. And some authors capture the true essence of the ancient technique quite well.

Firstly, all the experts your read or listen to, would tell you to not rush the process. There's no hurry to expert the breathing technique and get to the 'harder' poses. You should take as much time as your body requires to adhere to the new style of breathing.

After years of incorrect breathing, you cannot force all your organs to adjust to the yoga breath at once. It is like letting light enter a dark room from a small opening and letting the people residing in there adjust their eyes accordingly. The joy and the relief that your mind and body derive from deep breathing will automatically allow you to become accustomed to it fairly soon.

Patience will take you a long way on the journey as a yogi. It may solve a lot of problems generally in life as well. But since we mostly don't know how to increase patience, yoga can be used as an effective measure.

Nature never rushes anything. The sun rises at its own set time. The night falls exactly when it is supposed to. Not a minute late, nor a minute early.

Imagine having that kind of punctuality in your life. It would solve a lot of problems, wouldn't it? But the interesting thing to notice here is that we're relating punctuality to patience, something that would seem quite ironic to many people. Well, ironical or not, it is a lot more reassuring to patiently believe in the timings of things rather than stressing about running out of time.

Look at it this way. The sun knows that nobody can replace it. It has a unique role in nature and that role is extremely well-designed, clearly defined. So, it rises with all its confidence and glory, exactly when it is expected to.

Yoga requires you to think that you're a part, an extension of the same nature. Hence, you're not just irreplaceable but also extremely special. Nature would itself take care of you if you just synchronize your breathing with its breath.

Getting back to the technical parts, Indra Devi, the author of Yoga For You suggests that you first familiarize your lungs with a deeper breath than they're currently used to. For this, she recommends observing a sleeping person to noticing how the breathing also becomes more deeper as the person falls deeper into sleep.

For some weeks, you can try to consciously deepen your breath throughout the day. Try to replicate the relaxed breathing style of a sleeping person. At first, you may do this for brief moments and then extend the duration until you start breathing more deeply without even noticing it.

Once you're comfortable with breathing in this manner, you can actually attempt what you would call your first yoga breath. About this, Indra Devi writes:

'The spine should be straight, the head erect, hands on knees, eyes closed. Now concentrate at the pharyngeal space at the back wall of your mouth and, slightly contracting its muscles, begin to draw in the air through that space as if you were using a suction pump. Do it slowly and steadily, letting the pumping sound be clearly heard. Don't use the nostrils; remember that they remain inactive during the entire respiration process.'

To clear this confusion, let's make one thing very clear. It is always more beneficial to breathe in through the nose as compared to the mouth. The scientific explanation for this is that when you breathe through your nostrils, the air is cleansed, moistened, and also warmed up, something that doesn't happen in case you inhale through the mouth.

Even in the text above, Indra Devi is not telling you to breathe through the mouth instead of the nose. No, certainly not. That would go against the very principle of yoga breath.

By telling you to keep the nostrils motionless, the author wants you to inhale from deep within your body. Mostly, we just use the sensory organs or the upper chest muscles in the respiratory process. To fully benefit from the diaphragm breathing you must engage the parts lying dormant like they were placed inside your body by mistake.

These words may sound a bit harsh, but the truth is our lower lungs mostly starve for some oxygen. And the problem begins right at the start when we breathe in the air like we're in a rush. We inhale quite forcefully and then immediately exhale as if it was some kind of mistake.

Continuing the passage from Yoga For You that we interrupted earlier:

'When inhaling let your ribs expand sideways like an accordion--beginning with the lower ones, of course. Remember the chest and shoulders should remain motionless. The entire inhalation should be done gently and effortlessly.'

Does this sound too complicated to you? Well, remember the author's insistence that you just observe and get used to longer breaths for a few weeks before trying this? She was obviously advising you to prepare you for the first proper yoga breath.

But if you just want some instant relief, you're better off sticking to more basic approaches like Phelan's. Just remember to expand the ribcage and abdomen when you inhale and contract it back to the normal position when you exhale. A common mistake is to raise the shoulders or upper part of the chest assuming this would allow you to breathe deeper.

That is not entirely true. Think of it as making more space for prana inside your lungs and the rest of the body. You're not going to exert any part or organ when you take in the air from the environment.

However, when you exhale, let it be a little more forceful than the inhale. Just as much as to make the sigh of exhalation audible. A gradual, prolonged, and peaceful sigh which takes all your exhaustion and fatigue with it as it leaves your body.

At first, it would suffice to breathe in as much air as you feel comfortable. You can gradually increase this by a few moments until you feel like you have reached the full breath. If you need to determine a precise duration for the inhale and exhale, you can make a mental note to breathe in and out for about 6 heartbeats each.

This is slightly slower than the normal breathing rate. As you develop a rhythmic pattern, you can slowly feel the tension leave your body. The mind, the muscles, and the limbs become more relaxed.

While these authors explain the technical aspects, we would like to share a more personal explanation of what the first yoga breath feels like. If we stay it is a life-altering experience, it wouldn't be an overstatement. Metaphorically speaking, you're reborn as you become aware of the prana entering your body.

Imagine living in an urban settlement where there's always a lot of traffic. Cars honking, air pollution, congested streets, and chaotic scenes all around. Residing in such a busy town or city leaves you with no option but to embrace the noisy and crowded environment.

Suddenly, you come across a mysterious door and as soon as you open it, you're met with a light, refreshing breeze. As you take a few steps forward, feeling the soft grass beneath your feet, you can hear a waterfall in the distance. On a tree nearby, birds are singing a soft, melodious song that seems as soothing as a lullaby.

That sounds like a scene straight out of a fairytale, right? The fresh air in contrast to the smoke and dirt. The chirping of birds instead of unpleasant screeching of cars and bikes. In short, a sudden transition from a nightmarish place to somewhere that resembles the idea of paradise.

The clarity that a deep breath gives you is similar to the fresh air you breathe after living in pollution for a while. You start being more aware of your surroundings. The plants that you would earlier pass by without even noticing them start mesmerizing you.

You find every part of nature equally attractive. The frustration turns to acceptance. Gradually, with more practice, a newfound mental peace takes over.

This peace reflects in your glowing face and your calm demeanor. People start noticing the change in your mood and attitude. But the biggest difference is felt by oneself, like the mind has been cleared of some heavy for allowing clearer thinking and better performance.

Prana, the life force mingles with your blood and flows through the veins, spreading its healing power all over the body. If you have a strong belief in the spiritual power of the exercise, it works even better. You feel like your life purpose has been achieved by mingling with the energy of the universe.

In the introduction to the breathing exercises mentioned in Yoga and Nutrition, Kareen Zebroff presents an interesting view about the importance of breathing. We all obviously know that breathing is important for survival but for some reason, we focus on other necessities more. For example, we're more concerned about the quality of food we eat than the air we breathe in.

But Zebroff reminds us that a person can survive without food for a few days but survival without breath is limited to just a few moments. It seems like nature gives us a clear signal about prioritizing our respiratory health but we choose to ignore it. We would devise elaborate diet plans but seldom deem it necessary to work on our breathing technique.

As a result, we're found lamenting about our fitness routines not showing satisfactory results. We don't realize that we're expecting miraculous results despite ignoring the most important aspect of our mental and physical health. In fact, sacrificing our favorite food items and still not achieving the fitness goals we set puts us in a worse-off position than we were earlier.

Well, you could say it's nothing at all, or you could say it's everything you ever wanted in your life. It depends on the perspective. It also depends on the priorities you have in your life.

It's not a materialistic practice that would multiply your wealth or increase your fame. So someone who is driven by such motives might feel like it's a time-waster. After all, with such busy schedules, who really wants to just sit and breathe for a while?

Now, the other perspective. Let's begin by asking ourselves what is the main requirement for worldly success? How can you achieve your goals faster and more easily?

A few things that might come to your mind would be to learn more skills, work more, learn to use your time more efficiently, etc. Interestingly, all these things have one thing in common. They require greater mental strength.

The implementation of any goal starts from an idea. Getting great ideas and devising strategies to realize your dreams require excellent thinking skills. And we all know that our thinking skills are severely compromised when we're under stress.

Some breathing techniques for beginners

Enrolling yourself in a yoga class is not necessary to get started with the basic techniques. You can learn these at home with some great resources available online and in the form of some classic yoga books. Just try to keep things simple at first and enjoy the feeling that you experience whenever you try something new.

For pranayama or yoga breathing, you don't really have to get into a specific position. You can do it however you feel comfortable i.e while laying down, sitting, or standing. The main purpose is to straighten your back, be conscious of your breathing and try to use your diaphragm in the process.

Later, when you feel ready enough for the next phase, you can try some simple asanas that make this breathing more effective. Generally, the lotus pose or the frog are considered suitable for deep breathing.

However, other than the deeper form of breathing that you're supposed to get used to even when you're not exercising, there are several kinds of yoga breaths for specific purposes. For each of these breathing techniques, there are different yoga postures. Let us have a look at some of these in more detail.

The Cleansing Breath

As the name suggests, this exercise is meant to purify the lungs and the bloodstream. It requires you to sit in a cross-legged position, keeping your back straight. You may use a chair if you have trouble sitting in this manner.

Now, quickly inhale as much air as you can, pushing your abdomen out as you do so. Then exhale with the same speed and force, taking your abdomen back in abruptly. The duration for this whole process shouldn't be over one and a half or two seconds.

Repeat this ten times before taking a normal, relaxed breath. Then follow with repeating the cleansing breath another ten times. Complete with the regular yoga breath.

The Alternate Nostril Breath (Nadi Shodhana)

Again, sit in a cross-legged position. Bring your right hand to your face with index and middle finger resting lightly on your forehead while your thumb and ring finger are on either side of your nose. With your ring finger, close off the left nostril and inhale with the right one.

Close the other nostril with the thumb and just retain the breath for a few moments. Then, removing your ring finger, exhale from the left nostril (i.e the one that you didn't use for the inhale). Make the exhale a little longer than the inhale to empty your lungs completely.

Inhale from the left nostril this time and close it with the ring finger again. This time, remove your thumb and exhale from the right nostril. This completes one alternate nostril breath. Repeat five to ten times. You can gradually achieve a ratio of 4:8:8 with more practice.

The Humming Breath (Brahmari)

Have you ever hummed something to relieve nervousness or fear? This might be a similar mechanism for your body to relieve tension. It has a soothing effect.

The humming breath is just like the complete yoga breath except for this time, you make a humming sound as you exhale. You can repeat this three to ten times right before sleep. Ideally, it should be followed by **savasana**.

Breathing Exercise for Pain Relief

Body aches due to fatigue or any other reason can be extremely unnerving. They limit your physical activity and also cause great discomfort. In yoga, there's a breathing technique meant to breathe the pain away.

Quite often, we try to distract ourselves from the pain we're feeling. We either pretend it's not there or go on despite the difficulty, ignoring the protests of our body. Both these are unnatural and deceptive to your own mind and body.

Yoga requires you to do the complete opposite. You must focus on the pain and consciously work on relieving it. A yogi often uses the power of the mind for such healing purposes.

To try this, lie down comfortably with your back straight. Try deep breathing for a few moments. Direct the energy from the inhalation to the pain and with every exhalation, feel it leave your body with the breath. Be very certain that you can use all the prana in your body to eliminate the pain.

The Legs Up Breath (Viparita Karani)

This one requires a little more flexibility than the other beginner-level breathing exercises. Lie down on the floor with your legs up against a wall, creating a 90 degrees angle. Your arms should be straight on the floor, in a relaxed position.

Breathe deeply for a few minutes. If you're doing this exercise for tired feet, you can imagine dipping your feet in a red hot river as you inhale and then in a cool green one when you exhale. This can also help with swollen feet.

In case of sinus passage issues, you can try a slightly different variation of this exercise. Lie down on the bed crosswise with your head hanging slightly from the edge. Close one nostril and use the other one to inhale and exhale deeply for a few minutes. Now repeat with the other nostril.

The Lotus Pose (Padmasana)

You may be surprised to see that we're adding a meditational pose to this list, but we have a very good reason to do so. Whenever you meditate, the process involves the regulation of breath. It increases mindfulness and can be tried regardless of your knowledge of yoga.

For meditation, you just sit on the floor, in the classic yoga pose placing each foot on the opposite thigh. If you find this difficult in the beginning you may simply sit cross-legged. Then, take a few deep breaths and follow with normal (but relaxed) breathing for the rest of the practice.

Imagine something peaceful like the sun setting or a flower blooming gradually, one petal after the other. Do this for as long as it takes to relax your mind and body completely. Remember to keep your spine straight and your breath regular.

These are only a few of the various techniques included in yoga. But these are enough to give you an idea of the vast scope of pranayama. It is the beginning for such amazing techniques with numerous benefits, which will discuss in the next section of this text.

Overview

Whichever breathing exercise you choose for yourself, the starting point is to just expand your lung capacity. It is the building that you must enter to be able to choose the room inside it according to your liking. And you never know if you would even need to do something further as pranayama in itself is quite effective for many health purposes.

Every morning, just wake up and spend a few minutes filling your body with as much prana as you can. Like stocking up the reserve for the entire day. Then, during the day, whenever you feel like your breathing is going out of rhythm, take another few deep breaths to rectify it.

Or maybe at night, when you have trouble falling asleep and all kinds of thoughts attack your mind, you may practice yoga breathing again. In short, just think of it as a remedy for mental and physical stress at any time of the day. Doing only this would have unbelievable benefits on its own.

If we summarize all the explanations provided so far and try to define pranayama in a few words, it would be something like this:

Pranayama is a breathing technique aimed at the enhancement of your respiratory function. It is performed by making your breathing slower, deeper, and more relaxed.

The air you inhale contains nature's healing powers. This helps strengthen your lungs and consequently improve your mental and physical health.

BENEFITS OF PRANAYAMA

Let's admit, we're all very greedy creatures. The only difference is what we're greedy for. Some desire more wealth, others may want more fame, some people look for a bigger social circle while others have an insatiable thirst to visit every place they possibly can.

This greed can either make or break us. If you wish for something healthy, you'll be driven to work hard towards it and also gain a lot in the process. On the other hand, wanting something that's toxic for your mind and body can ruin everything.

Another thing to mention here is that we want things that would minimize our chances of ending up with a loss. We almost want a fool-proof guarantee that the solution provided to us would work a hundred percent. Looking at it this way, it seems like we tend to get a little unreasonable with our demands at times.

Actually, we don't. The desire is completely in line with the basic nature. If we're patient and persistent enough, we would start getting things on our own terms. But patience is something that our generation is always short of.

It's hard to quantify the benefits of something like pranayama. It's just like saying a good deed will earn you ten or twenty points. Or that a friendly gesture would yield a profit of twenty-five percent.

Adopting pranayama as a regular breathing technique is a service that you do to yourself. It is a favor that repays in more than one way. Some of the benefits are apparent while you don't even realize many insignificant ones.

Nonetheless, you will never hear someone say that the yoga breath has done them harm. Even patients with compromised pulmonary functions find it helpful in expanding the capacity of their lungs. The best part is that it costs absolutely nothing to get started. No equipment, no training, and not even a guide or expert.

The resources available on the internet are sufficient for new followers. Most influencers also include the necessary precautions according to your age or medical condition in their videos and articles. Apart from that, there are platforms to engage with yoga experts online.

Another thing that favors yoga breath over other similar techniques is that it has proven benefits for the longest period. It is one of the most ancient techniques used for breath regulation. For something to exist for so long and still be fairly popular, it must have something special.

With absolutely no side effects and people feeling visibly better upon the very first attempt, it makes a strong case for itself. The skeptics can't argue with the fact that this simple technique is much safer to try than all kinds of drugs that offer similar benefits. In the current era, yoga has regained relevance once again.

Now, what are these benefits that we're talking about? As we said earlier, one can't really quantify the advantages of something that is purely qualitative. But we'll try to gather as much information as we possibly can to explain how pranayama works so miraculously well for our mind and body.

Benefits for mental health

First and foremost, pranayama increases the synchronization between your mind and body. Naturally, this makes your reflexes act faster. The coordination between your thoughts and actions is improved.

Overthinking is one of the most common mental health issues these days. Your mind is occupied with so many thoughts and ideas simultaneously, throughout the day. Being so engrossed in your thoughts affects your productivity as well.

Furthermore, it slows down the decision-making process. Overthinking is also the main cause of chronic stress. So, by eliminating this root cause of so many problems, pranayama does wonders for your mental health.

But the most amazing part is the effect it has on patients suffering from anxiety or depression. The difference you feel within a few practices is so pleasantly refreshing. It finally allows for some relief from the gloom and despair.

This positive effect has also been proven by research. An article published on PsyPost cited a study involving two groups to study the effect on the brain of those who performed pranayama against those who didn't. It said:

"The amygdala has been the most cited brain region in studies related to emotion processing. This structure is part of the limbic system and has been particularly associated with negative emotions . . . We found that changes in the amygdala activity were correlated with changes in negative affect," Novaes and colleagues report.

The team further stated:

"In line with this hypothesis," the researchers say, "it has been suggested that the practice of meditation is associated with decreased activity in the amygdala in response to emotional stimuli, besides suggesting the influence of meditation particularly in the insula, ACC, and thalamus. Therefore, bottom-up models of emotion regulation seem to better fit the observed brain changes related to contemplative practices, such as meditation and pranayama."

If you build a routine around the yoga breath, you also get to enjoy greater discipline in life. You become a better judge of when you have reached your limit and need to relax. This allows you to take better care of your needs.

If you're a student, you'll see that this practice has made it easier to memorize and remember things. If you're a working professional, you'll feel more confident in day-to-day choices. In short, there will be a significant improvement in your mental abilities.

Benefits for physical health

A plant grows much better when it is nourished right. Similarly, you can help your body perform better by taking in more prana. It is nourishment for your mind, body, and soul.

The physical health benefits of pranayama include relief from hypertension and a lesser chance of developing cardiovascular diseases. More obvious benefits, just like any other exercise would include the regulation of weight and feeling more active. This technique is also helpful in improving digestion and boosting your overall immunity.

Apart from that, as the exercise strengthens your respiratory system, the flow of oxygen to all the organs is improved. Hence, the function of the other systems in the body is also enhanced. The muscular tension is released making your body much stronger.

These days, we do so much to get glowing and radiant skin. From laser treatments to painful home remedies, we put in so much hard work to make our skin appear fresher. But the truth is, this can be achieved with very little effort, just by incorporating yoga breath into your life.

So yes, healthier skin is another amazing benefit of pranayama. Since it purifies your bloodstream too, you can feel the effects on the physical appearance. The best part is, it's an entirely organic way of improving your skin.

The Fit Indian explains the various scientific reasons behind the skin glow in the following words.

· *Yoga provides a natural glow to the skin by flushing out toxins from the body. It also helps in regulating the digestive and excretory system that helps the internal purification system to work in a better way.*

· The soothing yoga poses help in relaxing the mind and the body and reduces stress. Stress can make your skin appear dull, tired, and worn out. Yoga rejuvenates and revitalizes the skin and makes it blemish-free by cutting down stress level.

· Allergies or impure blood can lead to infections, boils, and pimples. Yoga helps in healing skin infections and allergies by maintaining proper blood circulation and flushing out toxins from the blood.

· Yoga promotes restful sleep. Lack of restful sleep can make your skin lose its natural shine and luster.

· Yoga helps the skin to become tight and firm and gives it a natural lift thereby reducing wrinkles and fine lines.

Other than that, your body posture improves greatly. This helps in avoiding body aches related to improper postures. The yoga postures for pranayama and meditations usually require you to sit cross-legged, preferably on the floor.

Many of us aren't used to floor seating arrangements anymore. But this habit has several health benefits that we're missing out on. The pose for meditation ensures that your spine stays erect all the time.

Spiritual benefits

This one is a little trickier to understand. Despite reading all the arguments in its favor, a beginner would still be skeptical about a mere breathing exercise being touted as a way to connect with nature. Nature, which is in most faiths a superior, untouchable, divine entity.

Although this is a sensitive topic that requires an extensive debate, there are some basics that we can establish here for you, right now. You see, we seldom think that we can be an extension of that same divine energy. We're sinful, broken, or maybe even averse to religion.

But to consider yourself worthy of being counted among the miracles of nature is also a form of self-love. It's a form of respect for yourself, an honor of sorts. This instantly makes it seem easier to communicate with the universe.

You may not have supernatural powers, but you don't need those to understand the language that nature speaks. It requires no words, no gestures. The messages are conveyed from soul to soul, in a language they learned much before physical existence came into being.

Another aspect is that spending time with yourself makes you self-aware. So, while you're simply sitting by yourself, taking some deep breaths, you're getting closer to your truer self. The way you were originally made, without any impurities from this world.

Moreover, pranayama restores your belief in the goodness of nature. When you feel the positive effects on your mind and body, you automatically become closer to the divine energy. You become more aware of the way nature works and become more appreciative of it.

Benefits for emotional health

Try telling somebody that you're emotionally unwell. Would it be taken as seriously as a mental or physical ailment? Or would it just be brushed off as mood swings?

Unfortunately, emotional health is the most ignored part of our well-being. It seems quite absurd because your feelings affect your overall health directly. Your immunity becomes lower if you're sad and depressed for long.

Alternatively, you may have noticed that your mood suffers whenever you're not feeling well. You're likely to be grumpier when you're ill or stressed. So, your emotional health should be given as much importance as the other aspects of a person's help.

Now that we have established how important it is, the question is what can you do to improve your mental health? What are the things that can make you happier? Some of the answers may include meeting friends and family regularly, managing time for your hobbies, watching a good movie, traveling, etc. Doing things that make you happy will make you feel a lot better momentarily.

But as soon as that leisure time is over and you're back to the routine, there is a vacuum. In fact, now you also have to deal with the withdrawal symptoms after having such a good time. So, why not incorporate something in your routine that would provide more long-lasting results?

Just by including yoga breath in your routine, you're doing a great service to your emotional health. For example, in the text above, you read about how pranayama puts you in sync with nature. So, having so many other companions from the stars in the sky to the flowers in the garden would definitely make you feel less lonely.

The regulation of emotions through pranayama also helps improve your social relations. There are positive behavioral changes due to improved overall health. Hence, it provides additional benefits like enhancing your confidence and contentment.

Below is a relevant excerpt from an online article to summarize and conclude all these types of health benefits.

'In summary, this review postulates that mind-body exercise such as yoga couples sustained muscular activity with internally directed focus, producing a temporary self-contemplative mental state. It also triggers neurohormonal mechanisms that bring about health benefits, evidenced by the suppression of sympathetic activity. Thus, it reduces stress and anxiety, improves autonomic and higher neural center functioning and even, as shown in some studies, improves physical health of cancer patients. However, there is a definite need for more directed scientific work to be carried out to elucidate the effects and the mechanisms of such effects of yoga on the human body in health and disease. Considering the scientific evidence discussed thus far, it is fair to conclude that yoga can be beneficial in the prevention and cure of diseases.' (Sengupta, 2012)

Benefits of specific breathing techniques

Previously, we discussed some specific breathing techniques suitable for beginners. Apart from the aforementioned general benefits of pranayama, there are some particular benefits related to each of those exercises. Here's a list of a few.

The Cleansing Breath

1. It cleanses and strengthens the respiratory system.

2. Resolves sinus issues.

3. Helpful against colds.

4. Improves digestion.

5. Reduces overthinking and strengthens the nervous system

6. Good for the function of the liver.

The Alternate Nostril Breath

1. Strengthens the mind.

2. Helpful against headaches and insomnia.

3. Long-term practice alleviates anxiety and depression.

4. Extremely refreshing for the whole body.

5. Calms the nerves.

6. Ensures better airflow in the lungs.

The Humming Breath

1. An effective remedy for insomnia.

2. Helps relieve stress.

3. Purifies the bloodstream.

The Lotus Pose

1. Improves thinking skills.

2. Relieves stress.

3. Improves posture.

4. Helps against respiratory issues.

The yogic lifestyle

The yoga breath is a preparation for a bigger and more special journey i.e the yogic lifestyle. From keeping the body clean and pure to eating the right food, from giving up violence to letting go of worldly desires, yoga is a lifestyle meant for intellectuals with a significantly high level of wisdom. You can't just connect with your higher spiritual self without showing dedication.

Modern lifestyles like eco-friendly living make you care more about the environment. You willingly change your habits to reduce the damage done to the environment. It gives you a lot of satisfaction to live more responsibly.

But it is more about you trying to return some of the favors that nature has done to you. It is definitely quite appreciable to realize your blessings and be more grateful. That is what these environmentally conscious lifestyles are about.

Yoga, however, is a little different. It is like a gift that keeps giving without asking for anything in return. In fact, as you move further up the ladder of yoga expertise, the benefits it provides also keep increasing. As we mentioned earlier, yoga is a gift that you give yourself.

If you have developed an interest in this area recently, you may have questions about living the yogic way. Let's help you get started with some expert advice.

Roger Gabriel in an article (titled *Living a Yogic Lifestyle*) for chopra.com introduces two kinds of yogi lifestyles. These are The Renunciate Yogi and The Householder Yogi. As the names suggest, one is about leaving everything behind and dedicating your entire life to yoga while the other one is about incorporating yoga habits into your daily life.

To become a renunciate yogi you have to move to an ashram and avoid worldly matters as much as you can. On the other hand, being a householder yogi allows you to keep living your normal life but also make improvements inspired by yoga. The list of such improvements shared by Gabriel in the aforementioned article is as follows.

· *Be kind to yourself, to others, and the environment, in thought, word, and action.*

· *Be truthful and honest, including with yourself.*

· *Don't take what isn't yours, including not wasting another's time.*

· *Don't waste your energy, that of others, or natural resources.*

· *Don't be greedy; take only what you need.*

· *Keep your body, mind, and environment clean and clutter free.*

· *Have desires, but also enjoy the gifts you have.*

· *Be disciplined, especially with your spiritual practices.*

· *Study sacred texts and practice inner reflection.*

· *Celebrate your Higher Self and listen to its advice.*

This might be a good checklist to start with. However, you must remember that the list isn't exhaustive. You can find guidance about the yama and niyamas in yoga scriptures but try not to do it too mechanically. Only by letting the energy flow freely in your mind and body can you achieve true enlightenment.

The relevance of Pranayama in recent times

As we mentioned earlier, yoga has become relevant once again. The stress that has been gradually building up for years now, is taking a toll on the current generation. The overall health seems to be in shambles.

The rapidly increasing air pollution has poisoned our lungs and bloodstream. Every year, there's a spell of highly toxic smog which results in pulmonary issues. Our system has been contaminated with impurities.

Respiratory issues lead to a build-up of mucus which can cause permanent damage to the lungs. So mucus clearance is really important to keep your respiratory system healthy. Pranayama does this job quite easily and also has variations for different kinds of issues.

Excessive workload and stress, fatigue and exhaustion, emotional instability are all common issues these days. People are too busy to try something too time-consuming. Hence, pranayama is not only relevant for its effectiveness but also due to its convenience and simple technique.

And of course, how can we forget its usefulness in the middle of a global pandemic. The lockdown woes are something that nobody was prepared for. Stress, boredom, and uncertainty can easily hamper your mental peace.

You need an activity to stay busy, preferably one that doesn't stress your mind and body too much. Pranayama can help keep you relaxed in this stressful situation.

Hence, just get on a yoga mat, inhale some prana and exhale all your tension away.

CONCLUSION SO FAR

We spend so much energy working towards our goals every day. We're constantly running after the next milestone in our lives. It's like we have a never-ending to-do list and we keep adding more items to it without even pausing for a while.

In this process, we often forget to replenish the spent energy. Soon, we start feeling like we can't go on any longer. We can't do much about the hectic lifestyle these days, but at least we can make sure that our mind and body is ready for the challenge.

The idea behind this text is to help you recuperate without much effort. It's never too early (or too late) to switch to healthier life habits. And yoga does not even restrict any age group.

Apart from that, it is genuinely concerning to see so many people lose their sense of selves so early in life. Focus and determination are key factors to achieve anything in life. If you lose these at a young age, it takes a long time to rebuild your life.

It is quite heartbreaking to see so many youngsters falling prey to health issues caused mainly by stress. Losing the zest for life is one of the saddest things that can happen to a person. So, we should constantly and consciously work on our motivation levels as well.

Our lifestyle is becoming lazier so the physical strength and endurance of the overall population are also gradually diminishing. Although any kind of exercise is helpful, if you can manage to adopt one that caters to both physical and mental health needs, it is an added advantage.

We understand that life today is as busy as it can get. Most of us don't have time to visit the gym or go for a jog regularly. Nor can we retreat to an exotic place frequently to refresh our minds.

But breathing is something that we do effortlessly. If we can make a difference just by improving our breathing technique, it is certainly not a bad deal.

The innocent, childlike part of us always needs love, care, and attention. But as we become too busy in our lives, we start ignoring the needs of this inner child. Consequently, a very natural part of us feels abandoned and depressed.

Any living creature would grow much better if you feed it with more love and care. Pets, plants, children, you can name any example and find this rule relevant to it. Your own soul should not be considered any different.

Lastly, we would like to encourage the readers to prioritize their health and wellbeing at all costs. All kinds of success would follow if you're mentally and physically healthy. And let the very first step towards this goal be your next deep breath.

BONUS: YOGA AND THE DAILY ROUTINE

So far, we've focused on pranayama as the foundation of yoga. If we look at the bigger picture, the breathing techniques are just a stepping stone towards more complex yoga procedures. Although the information may have seemed like a lot, it only equates to dipping your toe in a vast ocean that is yet to be explored.

To dive in completely, you need to be passionate about the subject. Of course, this isn't something overly technical that you can perform by reading a manual. But a methodical approach would help you set the right goals to reach the eighth limb i.e Samadhi more easily.

When a child is learning to read and write, the sole focus is to familiarize him/her with the alphabets of the language. Every exercise developed for that level aims to ensure that the first step of the child's learning journey is as useful as it can be throughout life. The idea is to establish a strong base for everything that's coming ahead.

Hence, learning providers always pay special care to students who have just started school. There's encouragement, unique and innovative methods, and all sorts of techniques to keep the interest alive. This is the most important stage that determines proficiency in that particular language in the future.

However, once the alphabets are learned efficiently, the next step isn't delayed much. Children are quickly taught to start making words and subsequently, small sentences as well. Nobody spends an additional year memorizing the same syllabus, without a good reason to do so.

Learning a new skill or technique is no different than starting school. No matter what age group you may belong to or how much experience you have in other fields, for that specific technique you're just a new student. So, you need to follow a similar trajectory.

The learning process mainly consists of four different stages. These are called Unconscious Incompetence, Conscious Incompetence, Conscious Competence, and Unconscious Competence. Sometimes a fifth stage is added to this list which is known as mastery or Conscious Unconscious Competence.

These names might sound a little intimidating but their meanings are fairly simple. Basically, it's a hierarchy starting from the beginner and progressing towards the next level until you become an expert. How fast or easy this journey is for you depends on the level of dedication you have.

Unconscious incompetence is when you're unaware of a skill or knowledge. You don't know what it entails, what is your capability in the area, and what are the limitations. In other words, you're clueless about it.

As you gradually learn more about it, you become consciously incompetent. This means that you're aware and willing to learn but require some time and effort to achieve the goal. You're working towards improvement.

The third stage refers to those who have become fairly competent in the skill. For example, in terms of languages, you could say that they have started speaking fluently. So they know where they stand and where to go from here.

Unconscious competence is the expertise that comes with experience. You don't even know how good you've become at something. But it's noticeable for the others.

The last stage would be about knowing your own competence. You get an idea about the level of mastery you've achieved by witnessing the results. You know that you're ahead of many and can now impart the skill/knowledge to others.

Now let's relate this hierarchy to pranayama. Did you know about it before reading this text? Have you ever tried it before? How was the experience? Answering such questions would help you decide your position in this learning process and would also make it easier to identify the next step.

If possible, you can divide the eight limbs of yoga according to these categories. This would make it easier to choose the right exercises for your level. Everything becomes a lot clearer once you set well-defined goals.

Coming back to the yoga breath, here's an example that you may use as a specimen. Let's say you're currently consciously incompetent. You do have some knowledge about pranayama but you're fairly new to the technique.

This would mean that your next goal should be to become consciously competent. You have to spend more time learning and practicing to increase the effectiveness of the exercise. Like we said earlier, you have dipped your toe in the water and have an entire ocean that is yet to be explored.

Using this metaphorical example, you need to understand that you will have to gradually increase the endurance of your body. When you jump in the water, your whole body doesn't get immersed at once. Even if the difference is too minor to realize, there's always a gap between the first part of your body touching the water and the whole body being underwater.

Just like hitting the water with too much force would feel like a near-crash, trying to master hard yoga poses would also be counterproductive. Experts always suggest modifying the postures in case you feel pain or discomfort. So the first thing to remember is that yoga poses are flexible and can be molded according to your needs.

When you are consciously incompetent, you may feel pressured to increase the competence. The wish to excel at something new is quite natural. Therefore, you must keep reminding yourself that with yoga, you're teaching your mind and body to be more patient and just live in the moment.

Set a routine that you would easily but surely follow. At this stage, building momentum and discipline is more important. Whichever exercise you choose, try to do it consistently and preferably at the same time every day. Make it a part of your daily routine.

Let's say that you find alternate nostril breath most comfortable and effective. You can set a goal to practice it for 5 minutes every morning. Continue doing it the same way until you start doing it almost effortlessly.

This would tentatively take about a month or two. The decision whether you can increase the duration or make it more challenging does not depend on doing it 'rightly'. It depends on how well your body is responding to the exercise.

Aligning your goals with the body's ability is extremely important. You can't rush the process and expect long-lasting results. This is more about 'slowly but surely' getting there.

It can also be quite tricky to judge your own thoughts at times. For example, if one day you suddenly do not want to practice, there could be two scenarios. One, that there's a genuine reason like being unwell, or second, the equivalent of the fake tummy ache that children get when they want to skip school.

New learners in any study or field are just like little children, enjoying the good parts and wanting to avoid the bad ones. But in this case, there would be no parents or guardians to send you to school forcefully. Being the adult that you are and your own teacher for yoga, you will have to make sure that you adhere to your set plans.

Continue with the same routine until it doesn't even feel like you're doing something effort-consuming. When the process becomes almost natural, you can increase the duration slightly. Then repeat the same patient but persistent approach with the new duration.

Understandably, this would go on for quite a few weeks. Even when you've extended the practice to a maximum of let's say 10 minutes, you will spend some time practicing it with that duration. You will try a new pose only when it won't feel like an additional burden.

Achieving Samadhi

Now that we have established that your yoga journey would be slower than you previously imagined, let's talk about the ultimate goal that you should have in mind. Achieving Samadhi, the last and final stage of yoga is not just about mastering a physical pose. It's a lot more than that.

Samadhi is when you let go of all the worldly desires and achieve enlightenment. It is often defined as the purest form of rest that one can achieve while still being alive. The only time when you can be more peaceful is when your soul leaves the body.

The literal meaning of Samadhi, to 'bring together' or 'collect' translates into the yogic state of being joined with the Divine. One becomes completely detached from the physical existence. All worries and sadness related to this world become irrelevant.

It is a well-known fact that yoga makes you more flexible. Think of this as your body becoming more fluid with practice. Like the ice that has been hardened and is gradually melting into its purer form i.e water.

You may have heard of stories in which a sage could defy gravity and lift himself in the air while being in a state of meditation. Or, you might have come across different myths in the folklore about yogis being able to perform some supernatural actions. Although the extent of your belief in these myths is a matter of personal opinion, as a disciple of yoga, this is the kind of blissful state you're aiming for.

For a layman's explanation of Samadhi, let's say that your soul meets its higher self, the one that is closer to the divine entity. You attain a level of spirituality that is extraordinary, to say the least. Nothing matters to you other than being in sync with the ways of nature.

Surely sounds like a desirable mental state, right? No work-related stress, no worries due to personal relationships. It would definitely solve a lot of mental health issues for any person.

The question is what does one have to do to achieve Samadhi? Firstly, you have to master the first 7 limbs of yoga that come before Samadhi. You simply can't accelerate the process or take any shortcuts.

Secondly, you must strongly believe in having a connection with nature. It may not be religiously-influenced, but you must at least believe in some kind of spiritual enlightenment. Without conviction, true divinity cannot be achieved.

Last but not the least, you must give significant time to yoga. Undoubtedly, the positive effects of yoga on the mind and body start becoming apparent just a few days after starting practice. There's no time limit to meet or any standards to meet before you can enjoy the benefits.

But Samadhi is a different game altogether. It can only be achieved by the most devoted students of yoga. Those who are constantly ready to learn and evolve according to the teachings of yoga.

So, your best chance to get closer to the state is to be receptive. Absorb all the teachings and remember the purposes behind them as you practice. Instead of remembering the health benefits only, try to find out more about the spiritual significance of the poses you perform.

Complex yoga poses

A yogi is a calm and composed person who inspires you to achieve the same level of calmness yourself. But the physical strength and endurance that this technique builds can also not be undermined. Naturally, the poses required to become that flexible and fit are slightly more difficult than the basic relaxing ones.

Previously, we have discouraged continuing with any pose that causes pain or discomfort. Now, we're talking about complex poses that would obviously not be very comfortable. This may confuse you about how much to push yourself and where to draw the line.

The answer, in simple words, would be that you won't have all the answers in the beginning. Gradually as your body adjusts to the new technique, you will become more aware of its strengths and weaknesses. The enlightenment in yoga also refers to realizations about yourself.

Learning yoga is like constructing a huge building brick by brick. You can't skip one floor and build the next one. You also can't be impatient or careless. That would weaken the building making it crumble even with a minor jolt.

The rubble would be of no use to you. In the case of yoga, the rubble is the damage that the body suffers if you're too impatient early on. The right approach is to start slowly and gradually make your way upwards.

Just like breathing techniques for different purposes vary, there are a variety of different poses for a person's requirement. Strength building, improving metabolism, resolving sleep issues, etc, all have specially dedicated poses for the purpose. So, if you're into the modern or western variation of yoga, just to benefit from its physical aspects, you can choose the relevant exercise without getting into the details of the entire philosophy.

Breathing techniques can also be tried in some complex poses once your body has adjusted to the new routine. You're told when to inhale and exhale to maximize the effectiveness of every asana. Let's have a look at some examples of complex yoga poses.

Advanced forms of pranayama

Quiet Recharging Cycle

The purpose of this exercise is simple, more relaxation and more recharging of the mind and body. You consciously allow the prana to reach every part of your body. This is performed while standing in a comfortable position.

Take a slow, deep breath and retain it for a few moments. Then exhale gradually, as you imagine letting out all the stale air in the lungs and replacing it with the inhaled prana. With this step, you just sent prana to your solar plexus, something you'll continue to do throughout this exercise.

Inhale again, and this time, retain the breath for a little longer until all the muscles become slightly tensed. Exhale while relaxing and directing some more prana to your solar plexus.

For the third time, when you retain the breath after inhaling, rise on your toes. Stay in that position as long as you easily can. Then exhale gradually, coming down as you send prana to the solar plexus.

While you inhale again, raise your arms and put your palms together. Retain the breath briefly. Then return to normal position slowly as you exhale, and direct prana to the solar plexus.

Inhale and bring your palms together in front of your chest (like when saying *Namaste*) and retain your breath again. When you lower your arms and exhale, more prana is sent to the solar plexus.

Finally, combine the last two movements as you inhale. While taking in air, raise your arms above the head and join the palms together as you did earlier. But this time, instead of letting them stay above the head, bring them in the prayer position in front of your chest, like the previous step. Then exhale and relax as you imagine sending more prana to the solar plexus.

For the unaware, the solar plexus is connected to both the adrenal glands and the lungs. Stress-related symptoms like nausea and vomiting are caused by rapid breathing affecting your solar plexus. So, this exercise relaxes all the nerves and organs involved in this process.

The Bloodstream Purifier (Sanskrit: Bhastrika)

DO NOT try this if you have a heart or lung ailment. Make sure you're medically fit to try this pose.

In Bloodstream Purifier, you deliberately accelerate your breathing to supply more oxygen to the lungs. Another name for this exercise is Bellows Breath. The name is derived from the action of bellows that is used to pump air into a furnace so that the extra oxygen would make the blaze more intense.

To perform this exercise, one has to sit cross-legged and take a few quick breaths. Then, inhale deeply and forming an O with short lips, exhale in the form of several short bursts of air. Then complete with some more quick breaths. This exercise should never be overdone even if you're completely healthy.

As the name suggests, it is meant to purify the bloodstream and has additional benefits like accelerating metabolism, increasing alertness, and improving overall immunity. An even more advanced form would be to do this exercise by alternating between the nostrils but not before you're an expert.

Exercises for the rest of the body

Head-To-Knee Pose

For complete beginners, there is a sitting position variation of this pose. However, the standing one has better results. AVOID if you have high blood pressure or a spinal disc weakness.

Stand straight with your feet placed together. Put your hands on the back of your thighs. Now inhale, and then exhale while leaning forward, sliding down your hands simultaneously until they reach the ankles. Keep your legs and spine straight in the process, drawing in the stomach.

Without bending your knees, touch your head to them. Now rise up slowly. Repeat these steps again.

This exercise is effective in reducing excess fat from the stomach and waist. It helps relieve constipation and also refreshes your face. Most importantly, it keeps the spine flexible.

Pose Of A Hero

What an impressive name for an exercise, isn't it? Already makes you want to try it before learning about it. Its benefits are also quite heroic as it improves inner strength and courage. It's effective in strengthening your mental abilities and calming your nervous system.

Moreover, it strengthens you physically as well by making your back, knees, ankles, and hip perform more efficiently. So you can actually perform like a hero both mentally and physically. However, you should not try this pose if there's an issue of varicose veins.

You're required to sit in a position that is half lotus pose, half the simple cross-legged position. Sit down with your back straight and bend your right leg at the knee so that the lower part is resting beneath the right thigh and hip. That is, do fold your leg but instead of taking it to the opposite side, let it lay on the same side.

Place the left foot on the right groin, like in the lotus position. Now place both hands on the knees with thumbs and forefingers touching together. Close the eyes and breathe deeply. Now change the position of the legs and do the same on the opposite side.

Pose Of An Adept

Again, this pose is great for both your mental and physical health. But it should be avoided if you have varicose veins.

This is another sitting position that you can try when you're fairly new to yoga. Sit cross-legged, keeping your left heel close to the body. Lift the right foot and place it on the left leg (typically on the space between the calf and thigh). Keep the knees as close to the ground as you possibly can.

Keep the hands on your knees forming an O with thumb and forefinger. Breathe in this position with your back straight. Now swap the position of both legs and repeat again.

YOGA LITERATURE

Apart from the yoga sutras of Patanjali, some books are extremely helpful in making yoga more effective. In this book, we have quoted generously from some of such sources. Here's a list of the same, as a note of thanks and appreciation.

1. Title: *A Beginner's Guide To Yoga*

Author: *Nancy Phelan*

Source: Printed book

2. Title: Yoga For You

Author: Indra Devi

Source: Printed book

3. Yoga And Nutrition

Author: Kareen Zebroff

Source: Printed book

Some useful websites:

https://chopra.com/

https://www.yogapoint.com/index.htm

https://www.doyou.com/

In this journey, you'll be your own teacher and assess your progress yourself. Performance evaluation would mean that you need to check what/how much difference is it making to your life. If it isn't serving your purpose then you can always try a different breathing technique from a huge variety that yoga offers. If it's working well for you, then it's time to up the game and reap more benefits.

Playing the role of your first guide in this subject, have tried to enlighten you about some other prospects of yoga. As evident from the discussion above, pranayama is a doorway to better mental and physical health but more advanced forms of yoga change your personality completely.

REFERENCES

39.3B: Types of breathing. (2020, August 15). Retrieved March 20, 2021, from https://bio.libretexts.org/Bookshelves/Introductory_and_General_Biology/Book%3A_General_Biology_(Boundless)/39%3A_The_Respiratory_System/39.3%3A_Breathing/39.3B%3A_Types_of_Breathing#:~:text=Types%20of%20breathing%20in%20humans,each%20requires%20slightly%20different%20processes.

Beisecker, L. (n.d.). Ask a Yogi: What Are Patanjali's Yoga Sutras? Retrieved March 09, 2021, from https://www.doyou.com/ask-a-yogi-what-are-patanjalis-yoga-sutras-57749/

Boundless psychology. (n.d.). Retrieved March 20, 2021, from https://courses.lumenlearning.com/boundless-psychology/chapter/introduction-to-sensation/#:~:text=Input%20from%20our%20senses%20is,in%20the%20process%20of%20perception.

Devi, I. (1959). *YOGA FOR YOU*. Englewood Cliffs, New Jersey: Prentice Hall.

Diaphragmatic breathing exercises & techniques. (2018, September 14). Retrieved March 20, 2021, from https://my.clevelandclinic.org/health/articles/9445-diaphragmatic-breathing

Ellwood, B. (2020, October 19). Four weeks of Pranayama breathing EXERCISES reduces anxiety and negative affect and is linked to changes in the brain. Retrieved March 20, 2021, from https://www.psypost.org/2020/10/four-weeks-of-pranayama-breathing-exercises-reduces-anxiety-and-negative-affect-and-is-linked-to-changes-in-the-brain-58300

Fondin, M. (2016, March 11). What are the 8 limbs of yoga? Retrieved March 09, 2021, from https://chopra.com/articles/what-are-the-8-limbs-of-yoga

Gabriel, R. (2020, November 12). Yoga Sutras 101: Everything you need to know. Retrieved March 09, 2021, from https://chopra.com/articles/yoga-sutras-101-everything-you-need-to-know

Gabriel, R. (2020, October 13). Living a yogic lifestyle by roger Gabriel, CHOPRA Global's CHIEF Meditation officer. Retrieved March 20, 2021, from https://chopra.com/articles/living-a-yogic-lifestyle

Gajendran, D. (2018, August 31). 15 best yoga asanas and PRANAYAMA for Naturally glowing skin. Retrieved March 20, 2021, from https://www.thefitindian.com/blog/yoga-asanas-for-natural-glowing-skin/

Hajar, R. (2018). The pulse in Ancient Medicine Part 1. Retrieved March 20, 2021, from https://www.ncbi.nlm.nih.gov/pmc/articles/PMC5965015/

Mandlik, D. (n.d.). Ashtanga Yoga - Patanjali's Yoga Sutra. Retrieved March 09, 2021, from https://www.yogapoint.com/info/yoga-sutras-patanjali.htm

Morse, C. (2018, February 1). The dangers of shallow breathing. Retrieved March 14, 2021, from https://blog.powerlung.com/better-breathing/the-dangers-of-shallow-breathing#:~:text=PHYSICAL%20EFFECTS%20OF%20SHALLOW%20BREATHING&text=Shallow%20breathing%20increases%20blood%20pressure,known%20to%20speed%20up%20aging.

Nair, M. (2017, January 27). Yoga isn't An all-Hindu tradition – it has Buddhist, EVEN Sufi, influences. Retrieved March 09, 2021, from https://scroll.in/magazine/827658/yoga-isnt-an-all-hindu-tradition-it-has-buddhist-even-sufi-influences

Phelan, N. C. (1976). *Beginners guide to yoga.* London: Sphere.

Sengupta, P. (2012, July). Health impacts of yoga and pranayama: A state-of-the-art review. Retrieved March 20, 2021, from https://www.ncbi.nlm.nih.gov/pmc/articles/PMC3415184/

Zebroff, K. (1979). *Yoga and nutrition.* New York: Arco Pub.

www.ingramcontent.com/pod-product-compliance
Lightning Source LLC
Chambersburg PA
CBHW060405080526
44583CB00012B/477